Matter and Energy

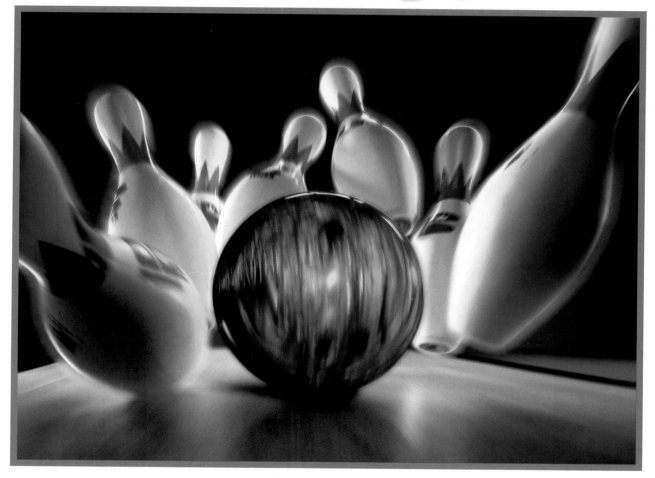

Developed at
Lawrence Hall of Science
University of California at Berkeley

Published and Distributed by **Delta Education**,
a member of the School Specialty Family

1012448
978-1-59821-785-8
Printing 6 — 7/2011
Quad/Graphics, Versailles, KY

The FOSS program began at the Lawrence Hall of Science as a science enrichment program. Over the past 25 years, with the support of the National Science Foundation and the University of California at Berkeley, the program has evolved into a total curriculum for all students and their teachers, grades K–6. The program reflects significant contributions of dedicated professionals in the classroom, their students, administrators, parents, and members of the scientific community. We acknowledge the thousands of educators who have given life to the ideas embodied in the FOSS program. We acknowledge and thank them all for their contributions to the development and implementation of FOSS.

FOSS © 2009 and © 2007 Lawrence Hall of Science Team

Larry Malone and Linda De Lucchi, FOSS Project Codirectors and Lead Developers; Kathy Long, Assessment Coordinator; Teri Dannenberg, Developer; Susan Kaschner Jagoda, Developer; Ann Moriarty, Developer; Kimi Hosoume, Developer; Deanne Giffin, Early Childhood Consultant; Joanna Totino, EL Consultant and Professional Developer; Jaine Kopp and Jenny Maguire, Mathematics Consultants; David Lippman, Editor and Program Specialist; Carol Sevilla, Publications Design Coordinator; Rose Craig, Illustrator; Susan Stanley and Carol Bevilacqua, Graphic Production; Susan Ketchner, Multimedia Director; Alana Chan, Nicole Alexis Medina, and Kate Jordan, FOSSweb Producers; Roseanna Yau and Leigh Anne McConnaughey, Multimedia Artist and Designer; Dan Bluestein, Programmer; Roger Vang, Programmer; Christopher Cianciarulo, Programmer; John Quick, Photographer

FOSS © 2009 and © 2007 Delta Education Team

Bonnie Piotrowski, FOSS Editorial Director
Project Team: Jennifer Apt, Mathew Bacon, Lynne Bleeker, Tom Guetling, Joann Hoy, Lisa Lachance, Elizabeth Luzadre, Paulette Miley, Sandra Mitchell, Cathrine Monson, Cyndy Patrick, John Prescott, Gary Standafer, Heidi Tyson, Nina Whitney

FOSS © 2009 and © 2007 Content Reviewers

David M. Andrews, EdD, Professor of Biology and Science Education and Executive Director, Science and Mathematics Education Center, California State University, Fresno, CA
Carol Balfe, PhD, Science Education Consultant and Former Research Scientist, Oakland, CA
Ellen P. Metzger, PhD, Professor of Geology, California State University, San Jose, CA

FOSS © 2009 and © 2007 Teacher Reviewers

Amy Edmindson, Centralia School, Anaheim, CA; Amy Hellewell, Bonita Canyon School, Irvine, CA; Bonney Waters, Two Bunch Palms Elementary, Desert Hot Springs, CA; Christina Lambie, Highland Elementary, Richmond, CA; Debby Palmer, Turtle Rock Elementary, Irvine, CA; Heinrich Sartin, District 2 Office, North Hollywood, CA; Jeff Self, Washington Elementary, Eureka, CA; Jennifer Faulhaber, G. H. Dysinger School, Buena Park, CA; Jill Garmon, Brywood Elementary, Irvine, CA; Don McKenney, Oakland Unified School District, Oakland, CA; Jill Miles, Sheridan School, Sheridan, CA; Jim Jones, Valley View School, Coachella, CA; Joy Peoples, Riverside School, Riverside, CA; Katherine Jacobs, Verde School, Irvine, CA; Kathy Albrecht, Heritage Oak School, Roseville, CA; Lauren Vu-Tran, Fountain Valley School, Fountain Valley, CA; Lillian Valadez-Rodela, San Pedro MST, San Pedro, CA; Lori Van-Gorp, Anaheim Hills Elementary, Anaheim, CA; Maura Crossin, Local District 4, Los Angeles, CA; Melissa Tallman, College Park Elementary, Irvine, CA; Nancy Lester, Newport Elementary, Newport Beach, CA; Pamela Rockwell, Anaheim Hills Elementary, Anaheim, CA; Rhonda Lemon, Danbrook School, Anaheim, CA; Sherri Ferguson, Brywood Elementary, Irvine, CA; Susan Liberati, Beverly Hills School District, Beverly Hills, CA; Will Neddersen, Tustin USD, Tustin, CA

Production for © 2007 and © 2003 Editions

LaurelTech Integrated Publishing Services

FOSS © 1993–2003 Edition Staff and Contributors

Professor Lawrence F. Lowery, Principal Investigator; Linda De Lucchi, Codirector; Larry Malone, Codirector; Kathy Long, Assessment Coordinator; Leigh Agler, Developer; Susan Kaschner Jagoda, Developer; Kari Rees, Reading Consultant; Carol Sevilla, Graphic Designer; Rose Craig, Illustrator
Contributors: Sara Armstrong, John Quick, Eileen Massey, Joanna Totino, Denise Soderlund, Laura Loutit, Eric Crane, Yiyu Xie, Marco Molinaro, Susan Ketchner, Joanna Gladden, Lisa Haderlie-Baker, Sandra Ragan, Cheryl Webb, Alev Burton, Mark Warren, Marshall Montgomery

FOSS © 2000–2003 Delta Education Team

Mathew Bacon, Grant Gardner, Tom Guetling, Joann Hoy, Dana Koch, Lisa Lachance, Cathrine Monson, Kerri O'Donnell, Bonnie Piotrowski, John Prescott, Jeanette Wall

FOSS Grades K–6 Revision © 2000–2003 Teacher Associates
Claire Kelley, Dennett Elementary School, Plympton, MA
Dyan Van Bishler, Clyde Hill Elementary, Bellevue, WA
Sig Doran, Clyde Hill Elementary, Bellevue, WA
Ann Kumata, John Muir Elementary, Seattle, WA
Kate Shonk, Pleasant Valley Primary, Vancouver, WA
Theresa Fowler, John Rogers Elementary, Seattle, WA
Andrea Edwards, Woodland Primary School, Woodland, WA
Deanne Giffin and Janet Gay, Bancroft Elementary School, Walnut Creek, CA
Jill Kraus, Hawthorne Elementary School, Oakland, CA
Brenda Redmond, Los Perales School, Moraga, CA
Catherine Behymer, Napa Valley Language Academy, Napa, CA
Alison McSweeney, Dennett Elementary, Plympton, MA
Helen Howard and Carol Strandberg, Mt. Erie Elementary, Anacortes, WA
Rondi Peth, Dawn Mayer, and Jeannette Beatty, Fidalgo Elementary, Anacortes, WA
Virginia Kammer, Fresno Unified School District, Fresno, CA
Henrietta Griffitts and Jackie Meylan Dodge, Mt. Diablo Unified School District

Production for © 2000 Edition *FOSS Science Stories*
Creative Media Applications, Inc.
Rhea Baehr, Writer; Michael Burgan, Writer; Robin Doak, Writer; Matthew Dylan, Writer; Emily Lauren, Writer; Matt Levine, Editor; Joanne Mattern, Writer; Dona Smith, Writer; Fabia Wargin, Graphic Design

Original FOSS © 1993–1995 Grades K–6 School District Partners
Kathy Jacobsen, Mt. Diablo Unified School District
Judy Guilkey-Amado and Alexa Hauser, Vallejo City Unified School District
Richard Merrill, Mt. Diablo Unified School District

Original FOSS © 1993–1995 Grades K–6 National Trials Center Directors and Advisers
Directors:
Ramona Anshutz, Kansas State Dept. of Education; Ron Bonnstetter, University of Nebraska; John Cairns, Delaware Dept. of Public Instruction; Arthur Camins, CSD #16, Brooklyn, NY; Winston Hoskins, Garland Independent School District, TX; Rhoda Immer, Siskiyou, County Office of Education, CA; Mildred Jones, New York City Schools; Floyd Mattheis, East Carolina University, NC; Alan McCormack, San Diego State University; Don McCurdy, University of Nebraska; Joseph Premo, Minneapolis Schools; John Staver, Kansas State University, Manhattan, KS; Brian Swagerty, Siskiyou County Office of Education, CA; Sandra Wolford, Colonial School District, New Castle, DE

Advisers:
Sara Armstrong, Heidi Bachman, Carl Berger, Donna Dailey, Robert Dean, Steve Essig, Rosella Jackson, Marsha Knudsen, Catherine Koshland, Samuel Markowitz, Glenn McGlathery, Margaret McIntyre, Shirley McKinney, Richard Merrill, Marshall Montgomery, Gary Nakagiri, Karen Ostlund, John Schippers, Dave Stronck, Dean Taylor, Judy Van Hoorn

FOSS © 1993–1995 Grades K–6 National Trials Leadership Partners
David Allard, Hal Benham, Diane Benham, Arthur Camins, Vicki Clark, John Clementson, Cathy Klinesteker, Karen Dawkins, Sally Dudley, Sheila Dunston, Steve Essig, Fred Fifer, Theresa Flaningam, Chris Foster, Robert Grossman, Cynthia Ledbetter, Charlotte McDonald, Karen Ostlund, Janet Posen, Carlton Robardey, Twyla Sherman, Gerald Skoog, Dean Taylor, Mary Zapata

Published and Distributed by Delta Education, a member of the School Specialty Family

The FOSS program was developed in part with the support of the National Science Foundation grant nos. MDR-8751727 and MDR-9150097. However, any opinions, findings, conclusions, statements, and recommendations expressed herein are those of the authors and do not necessarily reflect the views of NSF.

Table of Contents

Energy Sources

Energy makes things happen. Every action is caused by **energy.** For example, energy makes things warm. Energy makes things move. Energy makes sound and light. Energy is everywhere, and it makes things happen.

The Sun's energy shines on Earth all the time.

Where does energy come from? Most of the energy we use comes from the **Sun.** Energy comes from the Sun in two forms. They are **light** and **heat.** Light and heat are just two of the many forms of energy. Light energy and heat energy can make things happen. Think about when you stand in the sunshine. You can see the light and feel the heat energy.

Fuel

Energy is found in many different places. Anywhere energy comes from is an **energy source.** One source of energy is **fuel.** Fuel is material that has **stored energy.** People burn fuel to release the stored energy. How can you tell that energy is released when fuel burns? You can see light and feel heat.

Coal is used as fuel. When coal burns, the energy in the coal is **converted** into heat. The train in this picture uses heat energy from coal to boil water. The steam from the boiling water turns the train wheels. The steam train converts energy from fuel into **motion.** The energy in coal makes the train move.

Coal is the fuel used to make steam to power this train.

Natural gas is another kind of fuel. When gas burns, energy in the gas is converted into heat. The heat energy from burning gas is used to do many things. Can you think of some?

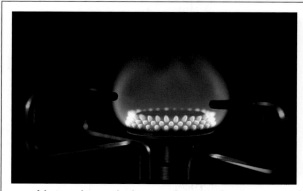

Natural gas is burned to make heat.

Oil, gasoline, and wood are also fuels. Oil is burned to release heat energy. The heat energy can be used to warm homes and make **electricity.**

Gasoline is burned to release energy to make cars and trucks move. The energy in oil and gasoline is converted into heat and motion.

Wood is burned to provide heat for homes. And wood in a campfire can be used to cook food.

Cars, trucks, and school buses use fuel to move on a road.

A family toasts marshmallows over a campfire.

Food Is Fuel

Everybody knows a slice of pizza or a piece of fruit tastes good. Pizza and fruit are examples of **food.** But do people eat food only for the taste? No, food is the fuel that makes life happen.

Food has stored energy, just like other kinds of fuel. In living organisms, fuel is "burned" to release energy. The food doesn't really burn, like wood or coal. The food is digested, and the stored energy is released.

Food is the fuel that provides energy for people.

Animals, including people, convert food energy into motion and heat. Sled dogs use the energy in their food to run, pull the sled, and keep warm. How do you use the energy in food?

All animals eat food to get the energy they need to live.

Chemical Energy

How does energy get into food? You may be surprised to know that food energy comes from the Sun.

Light is one form of energy. Light from the Sun shines on plant leaves. The leaves absorb the light energy.

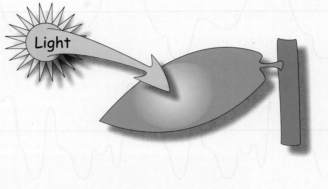

The leaves take up water from the soil and carbon dioxide gas (CO_2) from the air. They make sugar from the carbon dioxide, water, and light energy from the Sun. Sugar is food.

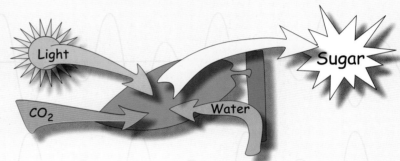

Sugar is a kind of chemical. The sugar has **chemical energy.** Chemical energy is another form of energy. It is different than light energy. Chemical energy stored in food can be released when food is eaten and digested. So really, it is energy from the Sun that keeps you warm, lets you run, and makes all your other activities possible.

Food has stored chemical energy.

Batteries

Electricity is a form of energy. Electric energy is used to make hundreds of different things happen. Electricity can make light. Electricity can make sound. Electricity can make things move. It can make things hot. It can make things cold. Electricity is a very useful form of energy.

A lot of electric appliances have a cord with a plug on the end. They are plugged into a wall socket. The wall socket is connected to a source of electric energy. As long as your radio or lamp is connected to the energy source, it will do its work.

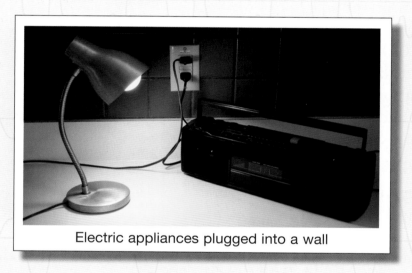
Electric appliances plugged into a wall

But what if you want to take your radio or lamp with you to the beach? There is no place to plug in a radio at the beach. But you can still play your radio. You just need to get a source of electric energy to go. This source is called a **battery.**

Electric appliances powered by batteries

A battery is a source of stored energy. Batteries are full of chemicals. The chemical energy in batteries can be converted into electricity. The electricity can be used to make a lot of different things happen. If you have a radio, electric energy can make sound. If you have a flashlight, electric energy can make light. The stored energy in batteries can also be used to do other things. It can start a car, power a cell phone, or drive a toy boat across a pond.

People use many sources of stored energy. Energy is stored in batteries, food, wood, coal, and oil as chemical energy. Stored chemical energy is converted into other forms of energy so it can be used. Useful forms of energy are electricity, heat, light, and movement.

Review Questions

1. **What is energy?**

2. **What are some of the different kinds of energy?**

3. **What are some of the sources of stored energy that people use?**

4. **How are food, fuel, and batteries alike?**

5. **What is the source of most of the energy used by people? Explain.**

Energy Conversion

Did you convert any energy from one form to another today? The answer is yes. Every second of every day you are converting energy. The action of lifting a pencil takes energy. The action of looking at a picture takes energy. The action of thinking about what to eat for lunch takes energy. Every action requires energy.

The energy for lifting, looking, moving, and thinking comes from food. The energy in food is stored in chemicals. As food breaks down in your body, chemical energy converts to heat energy and motion energy. Heat and movement are important forms of energy for staying alive.

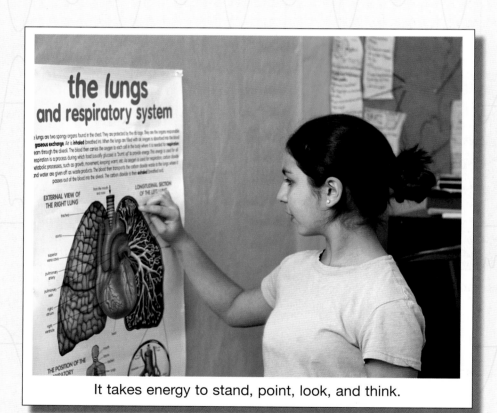

It takes energy to stand, point, look, and think.

Using Fossil Fuels

Do you know what a **fossil** is? You may have seen fossils of shells or bones. They are usually found in layers of rock. Fossils are the preserved remains of plants and animals that lived long ago. We know that dinosaurs lived on Earth 65 million years ago. That's because we have fossils of dinosaur bones that we can study.

Fossils are the preserved remains of organisms that lived long ago.

Oil, coal, and natural gas are called **fossil fuels.** Scientists think that fossil fuels started as plants a long time ago. For millions of years, plants died and piled up on Earth's surface. Over time they got buried deep underground. Slowly the plants changed into oil, coal, and gas. That's why they are called fossil fuels. They are the remains of plants.

Oil is a fossil fuel.

Coal is a fossil fuel.

Natural gas is a fossil fuel.

Fossil fuels don't look like plants any more. But they are made of chemicals. And the chemicals are full of chemical energy. Chemical energy can be converted to a useful form of energy by burning the fuel. Burning fossil fuel converts the chemical energy into heat energy.

What is fossil fuel used for? Transportation. Cars, buses, trucks, ships, trains, and airplanes burn fuels made from oil to move them forward.

Natural gas is used to generate electricity. The burning gas heats water to make steam. The steam turns **generators** to make the electricity used in your home and school.

Coal is used a lot in the Midwest and eastern United States. Coal is burned to generate electricity and to make steel.

Storing Electricity

At home you plug your electric lamp into a wall socket. The socket is connected to a **wire.** The wire is connected to a generator many miles away. The electricity coming from the wall socket is not stored energy. You are using the electric energy as it is being generated. The lamp converts the electricity into light.

Cars don't have wires connected to generators. But they have electric lights, radios, horns, buzzers, and clocks. Cars have stored energy in batteries. Batteries contain chemicals. The chemicals are different than the chemicals in food and fossil fuels. The chemicals in batteries make electricity.

Batteries come in all sizes. Hearing aids that fit inside a person's ear have tiny batteries.

Batteries that start cars are large and heavy.

Stored energy in tiny batteries powers hearing aids.

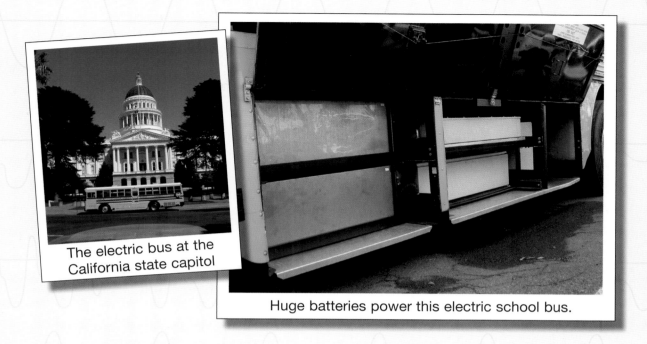

The electric bus at the California state capitol

Huge batteries power this electric school bus.

Batteries that provide the energy to drive cars and buses are huge. The Napa Valley School District in California has an electric school bus. The batteries take up most of the space under the seats. The chemical energy in these large batteries is converted into electricity. The electricity powers electric **motors.** The motors turn the bus wheels to move the bus. This bus never has to go to the gas station.

Sources of Stored Energy

Energy sources are everywhere. Apples, bread, and fish are all different sources of stored energy. They are called food. All foods have one thing in common. The energy is stored as chemical energy.

Coal, wood, wax, gasoline, paper, and natural gas are all different sources of stored energy. They are called fuels. One thing is the same about all fuels. The energy is stored as chemical energy.

Batteries come in hundreds of different sizes and shapes. They are all different sources of stored energy. The energy in batteries is stored as chemical energy.

Converting Stored Energy

Stored energy is useful to people when it is converted into other forms of energy. The most useful forms of energy are heat, light, electricity, and motion.

The chemical energy in food is converted to heat and motion in our bodies.

The chemical energy in fuel is converted to heat, light, and motion when the fuel burns.

The chemical energy in batteries is converted to electricity when a circuit is completed. Electricity is then converted into other forms of energy. The most useful forms are heat, light, and motion.

Look at the table below. Column 1 shows sources of stored energy. Column 2 lists the form of the stored energy. Column 3 gives the forms of energy that the source can be converted into.

Stored-Energy Source	Stored-Energy Form	Converted into
Corn	Chemical	Heat, motion
Turkey	Chemical	Heat, motion
Carrot	Chemical	Heat, motion
Wood	Chemical	Heat, light
Wax	Chemical	Heat, light
Oil	Chemical	Heat, light
Natural gas	Chemical	Heat, light
Coal	Chemical	Heat, light
Battery	Chemical	Electricity

Heat Energy into Motion

One important thing we get from heat energy is motion. The heat produced by burning gasoline in a car is converted into motion. The heat produced by burning fuel in jet planes is converted into motion. The heat produced by burning fuel in ships is converted into motion. The heat produced by burning coal in a steam train is converted into motion.

People and products are always on the move. Movement is action. Action requires energy. Every time you see a machine in motion, that machine is using energy.

Review Questions

1. **How are food and fossil fuels the same?**

2. **In what form is the stored energy in food and fossil fuels?**

3. **What forms of energy are food and fossil fuels converted into?**

4. **How is energy stored in batteries?**

5. **What is the stored energy in a battery converted into?**

Energy on the Move

Energy can move from place to place. We know a lot of light energy comes to Earth from the Sun. The sound of music reaches your ear from across the room. Electricity from miles away powers the lights in your classroom. A baseball hit too far can break a window. Light, **sound,** electricity, and **moving objects** are all forms of energy. And they all move.

Electricity is a form of energy. A battery provides electric energy to spin the **shaft** of a motor. The spinning shaft can turn a propeller. How does the electric energy get from the battery to the motor?

Energy moves from the battery to the motor as an electric current in wires.

Electric energy moves through wires. This flow of energy is called an **electric current.** Electric energy produced at a power plant is carried by wires to your home and school. You can use the energy right in your home to watch TV or run a refrigerator.

Energy and Waves

Some forms of energy move from one place to another as **waves.** A wave is a regular, repeating pattern. Some waves look like the waves on the ocean or a lake.

Other waves look like lines that are close together and far apart in a repeating pattern.

Sound is a form of energy. When objects **vibrate,** they produce sound. A **vibration** is a fast back-and-forth movement. A vibrating object pushes on air. That motion creates waves like the red ones above. The **sound waves** travel through air. They carry the energy created by the vibrating (moving) object. The sound waves hit your ear. The energy carried by the sound waves moves the little bones in your ear. You hear the sound.

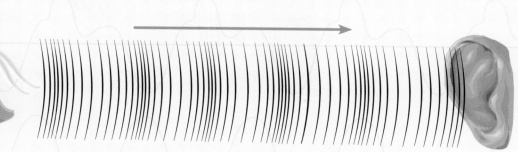

Waves carry sound energy from the bell to the ear.

Have you ever seen **water waves** crash on a beach? Ocean waves have a lot of energy. They can change the shape of a beach and wash away docks. Where does all that energy come from?

Anything that is moving has energy. Motion is a form of energy. **Wind** is air in motion. Wind blowing across the ocean pushes on the water's surface. The push makes waves.

Waves carry motion energy as they head for shore. Small waves don't have much energy when they break on the beach. But big waves have a lot of energy.

Small waves carry little energy.

Big waves carry a lot of energy.

Motion energy can be fun, too. Have you ever gone bowling? The object of the game is to knock down all the pins with the bowling ball. It takes energy to move the pins. Where does the energy to knock down the pins come from? How does it get to the pins? Let's see how the energy moves when you go bowling.

The energy in your arms and legs gives the bowling ball motion energy. The moving ball carries energy. If the ball goes straight, it will hit the bowling pins. The motion energy carried by the ball will transfer to the pins. The pins go flying. If you get the right amount of energy on the ball and the ball hits the pins just right, strike! All the pins go down.

Energy carried by a moving bowling ball knocks down the pins.

Review Questions

1. **What are three ways energy can be carried from one place to another?**

2. **How does sound get from a source to your ear?**

3. **How does a motor get energy from a battery?**

Summary: Energy

Energy is at work everywhere. That's because nothing happens unless **energy** makes it happen. Energy is behind every action. Energy makes it possible to do work.

Energy comes in many forms. **Light** is energy. **Heat** is energy. **Electricity** is energy. **Moving objects** have energy. Chemicals have energy. And energy can change from one form to another. Energy is everywhere and changing all the time.

Energy Sources

The most important **energy source** for Earth is the **Sun.** The Sun sends light and heat to Earth all the time. But there is one problem with sunlight. You can't collect it in a basket or bottle to use later. You can only use energy from the Sun while the Sun is shining.

But plants *can* collect sunlight for use later. Plants capture sunlight and use it to make sugar. Sugar is a chemical. Plants **convert** the Sun's energy into **chemical energy** in sugar.

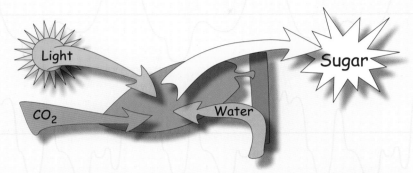

Plants convert light energy from the Sun into chemical energy in sugar.

Sugar is one form of **food.** Sugar can be stored until it is needed. Food is a source of **stored energy** that living things convert into heat and motion.

Energy is also stored as chemical energy in **fossil fuels.** The chemical energy in **fuels** is converted to heat, light, and **motion** when the fuel burns. Coal, oil, and natural gas are three kinds of fuel. The heat energy released by burning fuel can be used to power cars, trucks, and other machines.

Stored energy in food provides energy for people.

Stored energy in natural gas can be converted into heat when it burns.

Energy is stored in **batteries.** The chemical energy in batteries is converted to electricity when wires are connected to a lamp or motor. Electricity is a very useful source of energy. It can be converted easily to many other forms of energy, such as heat, light, sound, and motion.

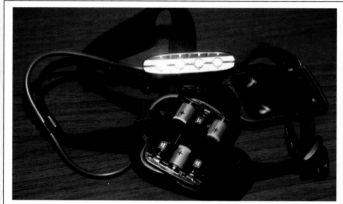

Chemical energy in the batteries is converted into electricity. Electricity is converted into light.

Energy in Motion

Energy can move. When you eat an apple, stored energy transfers from the apple to you. When you throw a ball, motion energy transfers from you to the ball. When you turn on a flashlight, energy transfers from the battery to the lightbulb.

Energy is carried from one place to another by **waves, electric currents,** and moving objects. A wave is a regular, repeating pattern. Some waves look like ocean waves. Other waves look like lines that are close together and far apart in a repeating pattern.

Ocean waves carry energy. You can see wave energy doing work when waves crash on the beach. And boats move up and down as waves pass under them.

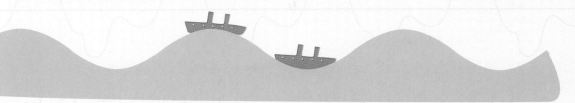

Energy carried by ocean waves is converted to motion energy in the boat.

Energy in batteries is carried to lightbulbs and motors by electric currents. Electric currents flow in wires. The stored energy in a battery can flow when wires are connected from both ends of the battery to the bulb or motor. When the wires are removed, the current stops flowing.

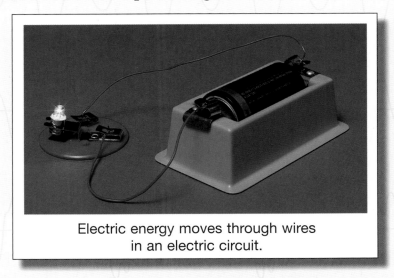

Electric energy moves through wires
in an electric circuit.

Moving objects have energy. When a moving foot hits a soccer ball, energy transfers to the ball. The ball flies down the field. When a moving bowling ball hits the pins, energy transfers to the pins. The pins fly in all directions. So remember this when you are running or riding a skateboard. You have a lot of motion energy. Be careful what you transfer that energy to!

Summary Questions

Now is a good time to review what you have recorded in your science notebook. Think about the investigations you have conducted with stored-energy sources and energy conversions.

1. **What is energy?**

2. **What kind of energy do we get from the Sun?**

3. **What sources of stored energy do people use?**

4. **When machines and living things use stored energy, what forms of energy is it converted into?**

5. **How is energy carried from one place to another?**

Vocabulary

energy

light

heat

electricity

moving object

energy source

Sun

convert

chemical energy

food

stored energy

fossil fuel

fuel

motion

battery

wave

electric current

Extensions

Math Problem of the Week

Power plants generate electricity used by people in the city. Electricity travels on wires from the power plant to towers. One tower can supply electricity to three poles. One pole can supply electricity to three blocks of houses.

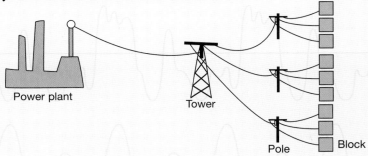

Power plant   Tower   Pole   Block

1. A power plant supplies electricity to five towers.
   - How many poles can receive power?
   - How many blocks of houses can be served?
2. The city wants to build 27 new blocks of houses.
   - How many poles will they need?
   - How many towers will they need?

Home/School Connection

Lightbulbs are rated by the amount of energy they use. The unit of electric power is the watt.

Record the watt rating for each bulb you can easily check. You may be surprised by the low wattage of the newer kind of bulbs that look like rope. Add up the total watts used by the lights you can check.

Older style   Newer style

Lightbulb location	Style	Watts

Reflection

Light is a form of energy. Light starts at a **light source.** The Sun is a light source. A lightbulb is a light source. A flame is a light source. Anything that makes light is a light source. Can you think of any other light sources?

Searchlights are powerful light sources.

Light travels in **rays.** Light rays travel from a light source in straight lines in all directions. Light rays don't curve around things. They just go straight. And they will go forever if they don't run into anything.

A candle is a small light source. It is safe to look at a candle. When light rays from a candle flame enter your eyes, you can see the flame. If light rays from the flame don't enter your eye, you can't see the flame. You can only see something if light travels from it into your eyes.

Reflected Light

Can you see the picture of a candle on this page? If you can, light must be traveling from the picture to your eye. But the picture of the candle is not making light. Where is the light coming from?

A candle flame is a light source.

Look around. Are the lights on in the room? Is there a window where light can come in? That's where the light is coming from. Light from lightbulbs and the Sun is striking the candle picture. Then the light bounces off the picture into your eye. Bouncing off a surface is called reflection.

A lightbulb is a light source. Light rays travel from the source in straight lines. Some of the light rays strike the candle picture. The light rays **reflect** off the picture. When the light reflects, it changes direction. But it still travels in straight lines. When light from the candle picture reflects into your eye, you see the picture.

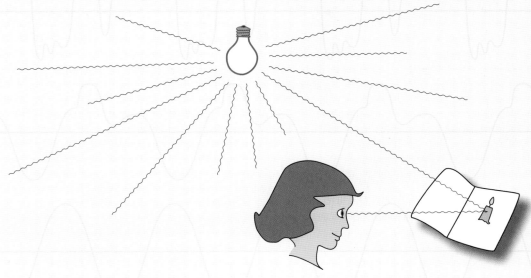

Mirrors

What do you see when you look in a **mirror?** Often you see yourself, but not always. You can hold a mirror to see things in other directions. In fact, if you hold a mirror just right, you can see objects behind you. It's like having eyes in the back of your head.

A mirror can show what is behind you.

Mirrors are shiny surfaces that reflect light. You can use a mirror to reflect light into your eyes. That's how you are able to see yourself in a mirror. That's how a driver can see what's going on behind her. And that's how sailors in submarines look around the ocean's surface. They use a device with two mirrors called a **periscope.**

A truck coming up from behind

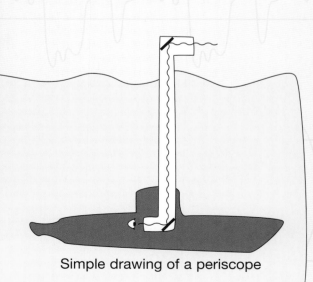
Simple drawing of a periscope

Mirrors can also be used to change the direction of a beam of light. Light can be directed around an object with mirrors.

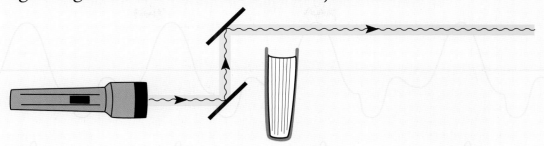

Light can be directed back to the source with two mirrors.

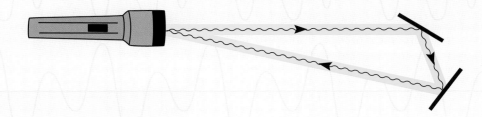

With four mirrors you can make it look like light shines right through a solid object.

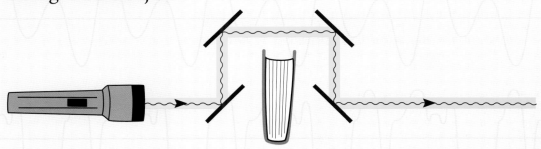

Two mirrors can be used to reflect light in two directions at the same time.

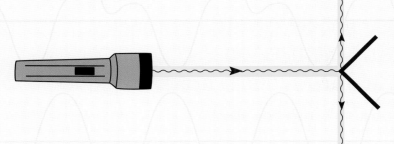

Other smooth, flat surfaces can act like mirrors. Sometimes you can see your reflection in a glass window. The surface of a calm lake can reflect light, too.

Smooth water reflects light from two people in a canoe.

Did you ever look at your reflection in a shiny spoon? Something funny happens. On the back of the spoon, you look tall and skinny. In the bowl of the spoon, you look small and upside down. Curved surfaces reflect light in interesting ways.

Spoon reflections are fun.

Review Questions

1. **What must happen for you to see an object?**

2. **What is a light source? Give three examples.**

3. **What happens when light reflects?**

4. **What kinds of surfaces reflect light?**

5. **What can you use a mirror for?**

Throw a Little Light on Sight

Sara's class was on a field trip at the Lawrence Hall of Science.

They were studying light. Sara was excited when she saw an exhibit called "Throw a Little Light on Sight."

A helper was standing by the open door.

Would you like to come in and learn about light and vision?

Yes, we are studying light in class.

Good! Let's go into this room. It has no windows and no lights, and I'm closing the door.

What do you see?

I can't see anything.

I'm putting two objects in front of you on the table. We will wait 5 minutes.

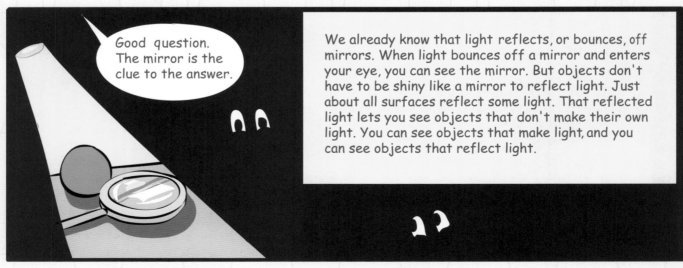

Tell me about how the orange looks.

Well, it is round, orange, and a little bumpy.

Now I am going to put some blue plastic over the flashlight.

Look, the light coming from the flashlight is blue!

How does the orange look when I shine blue light on it?

It looks black! It looks like an orange from a fairy tale. Why is it black?

It has to do with reflected light.

Different surfaces reflect different colors of light. The color of light shining on a surface affects how it looks. It is a fascinating part of the study of light.

What color do you think the orange will be if you shine yellow or green light on it?

That's a good idea. Thanks for helping me throw a little light on sight.

I'm not sure. I think I'll look for different colors of plastic when I get home so I can try some experiments of my own.

Sara tried some experiments at home. She got some clear blue plastic, some green plastic, and some yellow plastic. With these she could shine blue, green, and yellow light with her flashlight. With an orange and a lime from the kitchen, she was ready.

When she shined blue light on the orange and lime, they both looked black.

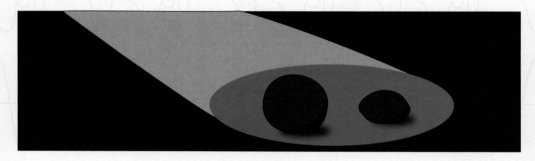

When she shined green light, the orange looked black and the lime looked green.

And when she shined yellow light, the orange looked yellow and the lime looked black.

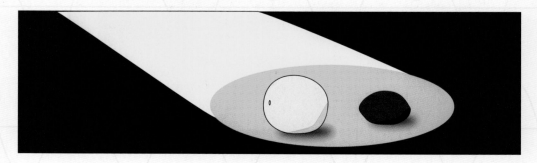

Sara remembered something she learned in class. **White light** is all colors of light mixed together. White light has yellow light, red light, green light, and all the other colors. A triangle of glass can separate the colors.

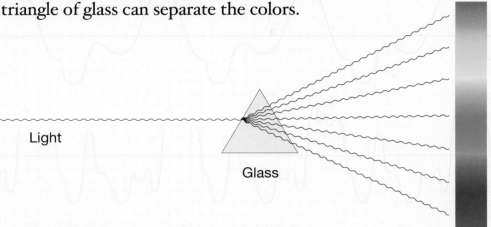

Light

Glass

When white light strikes an object, the object **absorbs** or reflects light. Objects like paper, snow, and cotton reflect all the light that hits them. That's why they look white. Objects like charcoal, pencil lead, and truck tires absorb all the light that hits them. That's why they look black.

When white light hits an orange, all the colors of light are absorbed except orange. Orange is reflected. That's why oranges look orange. All of a sudden Sara knew why the orange looked black when blue light shined on it. There was no orange light for the orange to reflect.

Sara thought, "I bet I can predict the appearance of a red apple in green light. And what if I had some red plastic for my flashlight. I could predict the appearance of the lime in red light."

Review Questions

1. **Why couldn't Sara see anything when she first went into the exhibit at the Lawrence Hall of Science?**

2. **Why did Sara's orange appear black in blue light?**

3. **Why did Sara's lime appear green in white light?**

4. **How will Sara's lime look in red light? Explain why.**

Summary: Light

Energy in the Sun can be converted into light. Energy in batteries can be converted into light. Energy in fuel can be converted into light. Anything that converts one kind of energy into light is a **light source.**

Light travels from a light source in **rays.** The rays travel in straight lines. A light ray will travel forever in a line unless it hits an object. When light hits an object, two things can happen. The object might **absorb** the light. Or the object might **reflect** the light.

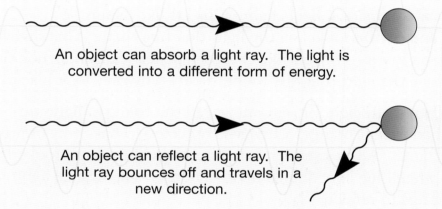

An object can absorb a light ray. The light is converted into a different form of energy.

An object can reflect a light ray. The light ray bounces off and travels in a new direction.

Light that is absorbed is no longer light. This absorbed light is converted into another form of energy, such as heat energy. Light that is reflected is still light. Reflected light bounces off an object and continues on its way. Reflected light travels in a new direction. Reflected light is not converted into another form of energy.

Mirrors

A **mirror** is a shiny surface. Light reflects from a mirror. A mirror can change the direction of light coming from an object. This is useful when the light is coming from behind you. A mirror can change the direction of the light so you can see what is going on behind you.

Hey, wait for me!

A flashlight makes a beam of light. A beam is millions of light rays. A mirror can be used to change the direction of a beam of light. Two mirrors can reflect light into a dark room down the hall and around the corner.

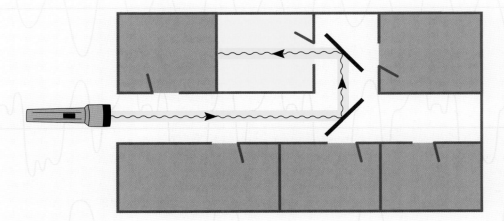

Most objects reflect light. That's how we are able to see them. Rays of light from a light source or rays of reflected light enter our eyes. When we see an object, we are actually seeing the light that travels from that object into our eyes. If no light enters our eyes, as when we are in a dark room, we see nothing.

Seeing Color

Light from the Sun and lightbulbs is called **white light.** But white light is really a mixture of all the colors of the rainbow. In fact, when you see a rainbow, you are seeing all the colors in white light. When conditions are right, tiny drops of water separate the colors.

White light is a mixture
of all the colors of the rainbow.

When white light strikes an object, some of the colors are absorbed and some are reflected. When white light shines on a red apple, all the colors of light except red are absorbed. Only red light will be reflected. When the red light goes into your eye, you see that the apple is red.

The apple appears red because it reflects only red light. Other colors
of light are absorbed by the apple.

What will you see if you shine blue light on the same red apple? The apple will appear black. The blue light is absorbed by the apple. No light is reflected.

The color of light striking an object affects the way you see the object.

Summary Questions

Now is a good time to review what you have recorded in your science notebook. Think about the investigations you have conducted with light sources, reflected light, and the appearance of objects in colored light.

1. Why does a green leaf appear green in sunlight?

2. Why does a green leaf appear black in red light?

3. How does seeing work?

4. How do mirrors work and what can they do?

Vocabulary

light source

ray

absorb

reflect

mirror

white light

Extensions

Math Problem of the Week

Gabriela has nine square mirrors. How many different sizes of rectangles can she make using her mirrors? She can use any number of the nine mirrors to make a rectangle. (You can use square tiles to help you solve this problem.)

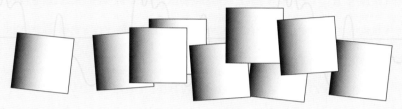

These two rectangles have the same dimensions, so they count as one rectangle. Record your rectangles and label the length and width.

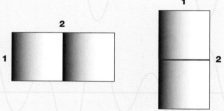

Home/School Connection

The Sun seems to move across the sky because Earth is turning on its axis. You can use a mirror to observe the movement.

Find a window where light from the Sun shines in. Position a mirror to reflect sunlight onto a wall. Tape a piece of paper there. Mark the center of the reflection. Wait 10 minutes and mark the center of the reflection again. Did the reflection move? Why?

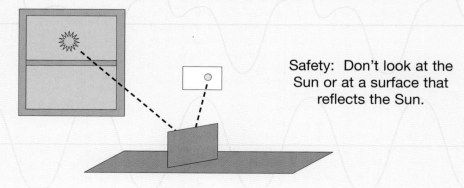

Safety: Don't look at the Sun or at a surface that reflects the Sun.

States of Matter

Just about everything you see is **matter.** Whatever you are standing on is matter. Everything you are wearing is matter. Everybody you know is made of matter. All those things you eat, drink, and breathe are matter. Matter is the stuff that everything is made of.

Solid Matter

Matter is found on Earth in three common forms or **states.** Matter can be hard like bricks, flashlights, and spoons. Bricks, flashlights, and spoons keep their shape if you put them in a basin, on a table, or in a bag. And they will be the same shape tomorrow. Bricks, flashlights, and spoons are all **solid.** Solids have definite shape. And they keep that shape all the time.

Matter can be soft. Socks, stuffed toys, and sponges are all matter. And socks, stuffed toys, and sponges keep their shape if you put them in a basin, on a table, or in a bag. And they will be the same shape tomorrow. Socks, stuffed toys, and sponges have definite shape. And they keep that shape all the time.

Liquid Matter

Matter can be wet and shapeless like water, oil, and shampoo. Water, oil, and shampoo are not the same shape if you put them in a basin, on a table, or in a bag. And they will be a different shape everywhere you put them. Water, oil, and shampoo are **liquid.** Liquids flow or pour. Liquids have no shape of their own. Liquids take the shape of the containers they are in. The amount of a liquid does not change, but its shape does.

Gas Matter

Matter can be invisible and difficult to feel, like air and helium. Air and helium have no shape. You can't put them in a basin or on a table. They will drift away. Air and helium are **gas.** You can hold a gas in a bag. But the gas will change shape to fill the space inside the bag. Gases spread out everywhere. The shape and volume of gases can change.

Small Solids

Solid matter can be in tiny particles. Flour, salt, and sand are all solid matter. But sand in a basin looks different when you pour it on a table or put it in a bag. Sand can pour. Is sand a liquid? No, sand is solid. The tiny pieces of sand are hard, and their shape and volume do not change.

Here's how to test a sample of matter to see if it is liquid or solid. Try to make a pile. If the matter will make a pile, it is solid matter. If it flows into a puddle, it is liquid matter.

Solid particles make a pile, but liquid does not.

Here's another test. Try to place a large nail on the matter. If the nail stays on top, the matter is solid. If the nail sinks, the matter is liquid.

A nail sinks in liquid but stays on the surface of a solid.

Review Questions

1. **What is matter?**
2. **How can you tell if a sample of matter is solid?**
3. **How can you tell if a sample of matter is liquid?**
4. **How can you tell if a sample of matter is gas?**
5. **How can you tell if a sample of matter that pours is solid or liquid?**

Opinion and Evidence

Two girls just finished the sponge activity. They were surprised that their 4-gram sponge soaked up 32 grams of water. That seemed like a lot for such a small sponge.

As they were recording their data in their notebooks, Teasha said, "If we had a natural sponge, it would soak up even more water."

"How do you know?" asked Kim.

"I just know it would," replied Teasha. "Natural things are always better. I would always choose a natural sponge. I'm sure it would work better."

"So you've never tested a natural sponge to find out if it can soak up more water than a **synthetic** sponge?" asked Kim.

"Well, no, I never actually did the experiment," admitted Teasha. "But it makes sense to me that the natural sponge would soak up water better."

"We could find out for sure," said Kim. "Let's get a natural sponge and test it. That should provide **evidence** about your **opinion** that natural things are better."

The Experiment

The next day the girls stayed after school to do their experiment. They had a new synthetic sponge and a new natural sponge. But there was a problem. The natural sponge was much larger than the synthetic one.

Teasha and Kim decided to cut three small samples from each sponge. The small samples would all be the same shape and same mass. They cut and trimmed and weighed carefully. Finally all six samples were exactly 5 grams.

"How should we soak the sponges to make sure it is a fair experiment?" asked Kim.

"I know," said Teasha. "We can hold the sponges underwater in a basin for 1 minute. That will really soak the sponges. Then we'll take them out of the water. We will hold them over the basin for maybe 30 seconds. Then weigh them to find out how much water soaked into each sponge."

"That sounds good to me," agreed Kim. "Let's get started."

The girls soaked the sponges for 1 minute

and let them drip for 30 seconds.

The girls soaked and weighed the first synthetic sponge. Then they repeated the procedure with the other two synthetic sponges. They did this to help them make sure their measurements were **accurate.** Then they did the same thing with the three natural sponges. They recorded their measurements in a table.

Sponge	Mass of sponge (g)	Mass of wet sponge (g)	Mass of water (g)
Synthetic 1	5	45	40
Synthetic 2	5	46	41
Synthetic 3	5	45	40
Natural 1	5	41	36
Natural 2	5	40	35
Natural 3	5	39	34

A Second Look

The girls studied the data. It looked like the synthetic sponge soaked up about 5 more grams of water than the natural sponge.

"Hmmm," said Teasha, "it looks like the natural sponge isn't better. At least not better at soaking up water. But you know what? I want to try one more thing. Let's squeeze as much water out of the sponges as we can. Then, starting with the damp sponges, we will repeat the experiment exactly. Then we will be sure our results are accurate."

Kim thought that was a good idea. They repeated the experiment and recorded these data.

Sponge	Mass of damp sponge (g)	Mass of wet sponge (g)	Mass of water (g)
Synthetic 1	7	45	38
Synthetic 2	8	46	38
Synthetic 3	8	45	37
Natural 1	7	41	34
Natural 2	8	40	32
Natural 3	7	39	32

"OK, I see now that the synthetic sponge is a better soaker upper," said Teasha. "The evidence is right there for all to see. From now on I am going to use synthetic sponges to soak up spills. But I will still use natural sponges for other things because they last longer."

"Are you sure?" asked Kim.

Opinion

Teasha likes natural things. She likes chairs made of wood. She likes T-shirts made of cotton. Her opinion is that natural things are always better.

When she and Kim were working with sponges, Teasha claimed that natural sponges were better. But her claim was not based on data and evidence. Her claim was her opinion. Opinions are based on what a person believes to be true, not on scientific data. Evidence is based on observation and scientific data.

In science, claims are tested with experiments. Experiments produce data and evidence. The evidence will show if the claim is true or not true. When Teasha and Kim did their experiment, the evidence showed that the synthetic sponge soaked up more water. Teasha changed her mind about sponges after she studied the evidence.

Review Questions

1. **Teasha claimed that natural sponges were better. What did she base that claim on?**

2. **Why did Teasha and Kim repeat their experiments?**

3. **Was Teasha's claim that natural sponges last longer based on opinion or evidence?**

4. **What is the difference between opinion and evidence?**

The Metric System

The **metric system** is a very easy system of measurement to use. Can you count by tens? Can you multiply and divide by tens? Then you can use the metric system.

Measurement systems based on multiples of ten were proposed many times in history. In 1793 people in France created the metric system. The French based this system on a unit they called the **meter (m).** Meter comes from the Greek word *metron,* which means "measure."

How did the French set the size of the meter? They made the meter one ten-millionth of the distance from the North Pole to the equator. They wanted the meter to be based on a unit that would never change. Today the meter is based on how far light travels in a fraction of a second.

North Pole

10,000,000 meters

Equator

The meter was then used to create other metric units. The unit of **mass** is the **gram (g).** The unit of **volume** is the **liter (L).**

Metric Prefixes

All metric units are based on the meter. The prefix can help you tell how big a metric unit is. The prefix is the part of the word that comes first.

millimeter	=	0.001 meter (one-thousandth)
centimeter	=	0.01 meter (one-hundredth)
decimeter	=	0.1 meter (one-tenth)
meter	=	1.0 meter
dekameter	=	10.0 meters
hectometer	=	100.0 meters
kilometer	=	1,000.0 meters

Length, Mass, and Volume

The meter is used to define the basic units of mass and volume in the metric system. Here's how.

Mass The basic unit of mass in the metric system is the gram.

One cubic centimeter of water has a mass of 1 gram.

Volume The basic unit of volume in the metric system is the liter.

A 10-centimeter cube has a volume of 1 liter.

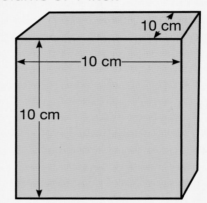

The metric system slowly caught on around the world. Seventeen countries signed the Treaty of the Meter in 1875. This treaty created the International Bureau of Weights and Measures. The bureau adopted the metric system as the worldwide standard of measurement. Today the metric system is the standard everywhere in the world.

Everywhere, that is, except the United States. The United States does not use the metric system. It is the only country in the world that does not use the metric system as its official measuring system. But even in the United States, the metric system is used in many areas. It is used in most scientific fields. It is used in many sports and recreation activities. And one day, metrics will probably be used for everyday measurement in your home.

Review Question

Explain how the metric system units for mass and volume are based on the meter.

Summary: Matter

Everything you see in the picture on this page is matter. Things that you can touch are **matter.** The chair is matter. The tables are matter. The water in the aquarium is matter. The fish in the water are matter. The plants are matter. And the air that you can't see is matter, too.

An office filled with solid, liquid, and gas matter

Forms of Matter

Matter on Earth has three common forms or **states.** Most things we come into contact with are **solid.** Solid matter has definite shape. The shape doesn't change when you put a solid in a different place. Streets are solid. Shoes are solid. Pencils, bags of rice, and pillows are solid.

Matter that has no shape but can be held in an open container is **liquid.** Liquids flow, pour, and spill. They spread out if they are not in containers. Water, milk, and tomato juice are liquid matter. Syrup, catsup, and glue pour slowly. That's because they are thick liquids. Liquid settles in the bottom of a container. And the liquid is flat and level on top.

Liquids take the shape of their containers.

Matter that has no shape and won't stay in an open container is **gas.** Most gases are invisible. Air is gas. Helium in helium balloons is gas. And natural gas can be burned to make heat. Gases move in all directions. You can feel gas when it is moving. Wind is moving air.

Measuring Matter

Matter has **mass** and **volume.** Matter can be weighed to determine its mass. The basic unit of mass in the **metric system** is the **gram.** One cubic centimeter of water has a mass of 1 gram. A paper clip has a mass of 1 gram. A train has a mass of thousands of kilograms.

Matter can be measured to determine its volume. The basic unit of volume is the **liter.** It is pretty easy to measure the volume of a small amount of liquid. All you do is pour it into a graduated cylinder. The milliliter lines will show the volume of liquid. Gases can be pulled into a syringe to measure their volume.

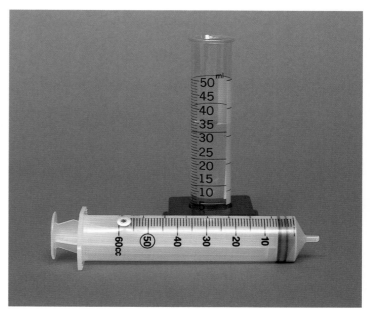

A 50-mL syringe and a 50-mL graduated cylinder

Evidence and Opinion

The work of scientists is to find answers to questions about the natural world. They use **evidence** to make sure their answers are accurate and correct. Evidence is based on many observations and careful measurements.

Scientists sometimes have **opinions** about the questions they are working on. Opinions are based on what they believe to be true. But scientists are always careful to base their answers on scientific evidence, not on their opinions.

Summary Questions

Now is a good time to review what you have recorded in your science notebook. Think about the investigations you have conducted with mass and volume.

1. What form does matter take on Earth?
2. What are the characteristics of solids?
3. What are the characteristics of liquids?
4. What are the characteristics of gases?
5. How is mass measured in the metric system?
6. How is volume measured in the metric system?
7. What is the difference between evidence and opinion?

Vocabulary

matter

state

solid

liquid

gas

mass

volume

metric system

gram

liter

evidence

opinion

Extensions

Math Problem of the Week

A 1-gram sponge can soak up 5 g of water.

1. How many grams of water can a 40-g sponge soak up?

2. What is the mass of a sponge that can soak up 150 g of water?

3. How many grams of water can a 25-g sponge soak up?

4. If you have a 40-g sponge, how many soaks will it take to soak up a liter of water?

Home/School Connection

Find five packages of solid food, such as rice or cereal. Also find five liquid containers, such as fruit juice or dishwashing detergent. Estimate the mass of the solid products in grams and the volume of the liquid products in milliliters. Then check the labels to see how accurate your estimates are.

Solid products	Mass estimate	Mass from label
Liquid products	**Volume estimate**	**Volume from label**

Change of State

ce **melts.** It changes from solid to liquid. An ice cube in a cup on your desk will change into water in about an hour. Chocolate and margarine melt, too. But they will not melt on your desk. You have to put them in hot water to make them melt. Wax melts a little bit in hot water. It gets soft. But a pebble won't melt at all. Or will it?

Solid to Liquid

What caused the margarine to melt? Heat. You put margarine in a cup. Nothing happened. You put the cup in hot water. The margarine melted. Heat transferred from the hot water to the margarine. The heat made the margarine melt.

Heat is causing this butter to melt.

But ice melts without heat. Why is that? Actually, heat does make ice melt. When ice is in the freezer, it doesn't melt. It stays solid. When you bring ice out into a room that is warmer than the freezer, it melts. That's because heat from the room transfers to the ice and causes it to melt.

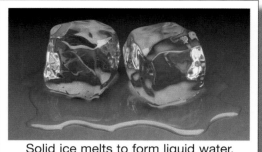
Solid ice melts to form liquid water.

Materials melt at different **temperatures.** Water melts at 0°C (32°F). When water is below 0°C, it is solid. When it is above 0°C, it is liquid. Chocolate melts at about 50°C (122°F). Candle wax melts into liquid at around 80°C (176°F). And yes, the pebble will melt when it is heated to over 1,000°C (1,832°F)! Have you ever seen lava flowing down from a volcano? That's melted rock.

Lava flowing down the side of Kilauea Volcano in Hawaii

Metals melt, too. Jewelers melt gold and silver to make rings and other beautiful things. Sculptors melt bronze to make statues. Iron and copper are melted to separate them from the ores taken from mines. Sand is melted to make glass.

Many things that we think are always solid will melt if enough heat is transferred to them.

Gold melts at 1,064°C.

Liquid to Gas

Puddles dry up. Wet clothes get dry. Raindrops on cars disappear. It seems like liquid water is disappearing everywhere you look. Where does it go?

It **evaporates.** When water evaporates, it changes from liquid to **water vapor,** a gas. The gas drifts away in the air.

Water isn't the only liquid that evaporates. Gasoline for cars is liquid. It is kept in tightly closed gas tanks. If the gasoline were left in open containers, it would evaporate and disappear into the air.

Here's an interesting fact. We breathe oxygen from the air. Oxygen in the air is a gas. But if you put a container of oxygen in a freezer that is −183°C (−297°F), the oxygen becomes liquid. Because Earth is much warmer than −183°C, all of Earth's oxygen has evaporated. It is all gas in the air.

What causes liquids to evaporate? Heat. When enough heat transfers to a liquid, the liquid changes into a gas. The problem is that most gases are invisible. It is very difficult to know if there is a substance around that is in the gas state.

There is one way to find out. If you transfer enough heat away from a gas, it will change into a liquid. Then you can see it. Have you seen any water vapor that changed back into liquid water lately? That's what a cloud is. When invisible water vapor rises high in the sky and cools, the water vapor changes back into liquid. And then you can see it.

Review Questions

1. **What is melting?**
2. **What causes matter to melt?**
3. **What is evaporation?**
4. **What causes evaporation?**

Particles

What is matter? We know matter is what everything is made of. Mountains are solid matter. A bread crumb is solid matter. The ocean is liquid matter. A drop of rain is liquid matter. Earth's atmosphere is gas matter. A bubble in a glass of soda is gas matter. All solids, liquids, and gases are matter. But what is matter made of?

All the matter in the world is made of tiny bits called **particles.** Particles go together to make everything. Particles can be thought of as the building blocks of matter.

You can't see a single particle with your naked eye. Particles are far too small. A tiny grain of sand is made of millions of particles.

All solids, all liquids, and all gases are made of particles. You are made of particles. Everything you eat, drink, and breathe is made of particles. Earth itself is made of particles, and so are the ocean and all the things living in it.

Particles in Motion

Particles are always moving. Particles in solids are stuck together. That's why solids have definite shape. But even though they are stuck together, the particles are vibrating and jiggling. Particles in a solid are like a bunch of people crowded together, jumping up and down.

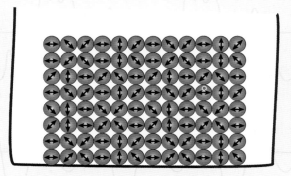

Particles in solids are stuck together.

Particles in liquids are not stuck together, but they are touching. Particles in liquids can push and slide past and around each other. That's why liquids don't have a definite shape. The particles flow past each other. Particles in a liquid are like a bunch of people close together in one side of a room. But all of the people are walking around here and there past each other.

Particles in liquids touch, but they flow past one another.

Particles in gases are not close to each other. Particles in gases fly around, crashing into things and bouncing off in new directions. Particles in gases fly off in all directions. That's why gases can't be kept in open containers. Particles in gases are like a bunch of people in a huge room. These people are running as fast as they can, bouncing off each other and the walls.

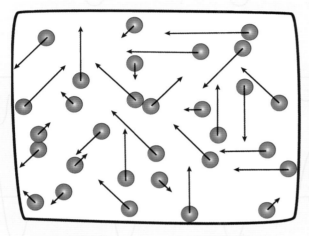

Particles in gases fly off in all directions.

Review Questions

1. **What is all matter made of?**

2. **How are the particles moving in this solid ice, liquid water, and water vapor?**

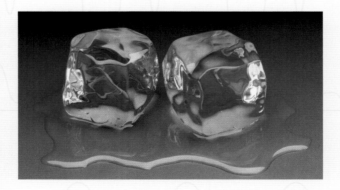

Reactions

Everything is made of particles. Particles combine to make **substances.** Water is a substance. Salt is a substance. Water is made of hydrogen and oxygen particles. Salt is made of sodium and chlorine particles. All substances are made of particles.

Vinegar and baking soda are two substances you worked with in class. Vinegar and baking soda have **properties** that help you identify them. Vinegar is a liquid substance with a strong smell. Baking soda is a solid substance in the form of a powder.

Baking soda and vinegar

Carlo did an experiment to see what happens when vinegar and baking soda are combined. He put solid baking soda in one cup. He put liquid vinegar in another cup.

Carlo put the vinegar cup inside the baking soda cup. He then put the two cups on one side of a balance and mass pieces on the other side. He added mass pieces until the system balanced.

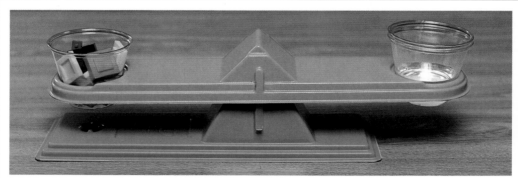
Mass pieces equal to the mass of the baking soda and vinegar

He then carefully poured the vinegar into the cup with baking soda. The vinegar and baking soda fizzed and bubbled.

Carbon dioxide gas forms when vinegar and baking soda combine.

What happened? The vinegar and baking soda reacted. During the **reaction,** new substances formed. Carlo mixed a liquid and a solid, and a gas formed. The gas that made all the bubbles was a new substance. Where did the gas come from?

The particles in the vinegar and baking soda combined in new ways during the reaction. One new combination formed the gas carbon dioxide. That's where the gas came from. The gas was a new substance that formed when vinegar and baking soda reacted.

After the fizzing stopped, Carlo looked in the cup. There was no solid baking soda left. He smelled the cup carefully. It no longer smelled like vinegar. The new substances had different properties than the starting substances.

Carlo made one more observation. The mass pieces were still in the cup on the balance. He put his two cups back on the balance. The system did not balance. The reaction cup had less mass than it did before. Why?

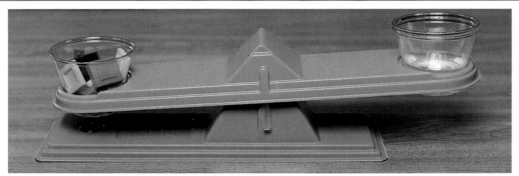

The mass after the reaction is less than it was before the reaction.

Gas is matter, so it has mass. When the carbon dioxide gas formed, it went into the air. Millions of particles left the cup and went into the air. The cup lost mass.

Millions of Substances

All the solids, liquids, and gases on Earth are matter. All the different kinds of matter are called substances. There are millions of different substances on Earth.

Particles combine to form new substances. Every different combination of particles makes a different substance. The particles rearrange during reactions. New arrangements of particles make new substances.

Carlo made a new substance by combining baking soda and vinegar. Other new substances can be made by combining other starting substances.

Review Questions

1. **How do new substances form?**

2. **Why did Carlo's reaction cup have less mass after the fizzing stopped?**

Summary: Changing Matter

Matter has mass and volume. Those two facts about matter never change. But matter can change. Matter can change state. Matter can also change from one **substance** into another.

Change of State

Matter exists on Earth in three common forms, solid, liquid, and gas. These three forms are called states. Butter, chocolate, and wax are solids. If you put them in an iron pan on a hot stove, heat will transfer to the solid materials. In a short time the butter will **melt.** When an object melts, it changes from solid to liquid.

If the heat stays on, the chocolate will melt. Then the wax will melt. And if the heat is high enough, the iron pan will melt, too.

Water is a liquid. If you put water in an aluminum pot on a stove, heat will transfer to the liquid water. The water will **evaporate.** When a material evaporates, it changes from liquid to gas. The gas is called water vapor. And if the heat is high enough, the aluminum pan will melt into liquid and then turn into gas. But don't try this at home. Stoves don't get nearly hot enough to melt and vaporize metals like iron and aluminum.

Melting and evaporation are changes of state. Melting and evaporation are changes to matter that occur when objects are heated.

Change of Substance

Remember when you mixed baking soda and vinegar? You started with a white solid powder and a clear liquid. When you combined them, the mixture bubbled and fizzed. The bubbles were caused by a gas. The gas was a new substance that formed when baking soda and vinegar combined.

Gas forms when baking soda and vinegar combine.

The bubbling was evidence of a **reaction.** During reactions, starting substances change into new substances.

Everything Is Made of Particles

Matter is made of tiny **particles.** Particles are far too small to be seen with your naked eye. Particles are the building blocks of matter. There are 90 different basic particles occurring naturally on Earth. All the millions of different kinds of matter are made from these particles.

In solid matter, particles are attached to each other. That's why solids have definite shape.

In liquid matter, particles are touching, but they can move around and past one another. That's why liquids flow.

In gas matter, particles are flying around by themselves. There is a lot of space between the particles. That's why gases must be kept in closed containers.

Summary Questions

Now is a good time to review what you have recorded in your science notebook. Think about the investigations you have conducted with melting and evaporation and how new substances form during reactions. Review what matter is made of and how heat affects particles when matter melts and evaporates.

1. How does matter change when it melts?

2. How does matter change when it evaporates?

3. What causes melting and evaporation?

4. How does matter change during reactions?

5. What is all matter made of?

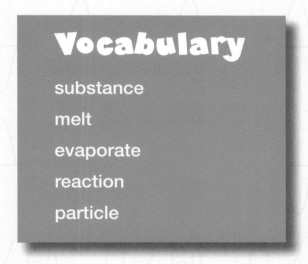

Vocabulary

substance

melt

evaporate

reaction

particle

References

Learning More about Matter and Energy

Start an Energy Toy Collection

Do you have toys that use stored energy to do interesting things? The energy might be stored in batteries, springs, or spinning flywheels. Some possibilities include model cars, twirling dolls, and windup animals.

Write Mirror Messages

Learn to write so that the writing can be read only in a mirror. One style of writing you can read with the mirror above the writing. The other you can read with the mirror at one side. Write messages to share with a friend.

Create Mirror Pictures

Create designs or partial pictures of objects that need a mirror to make them complete.

Look at Symmetry of Faces

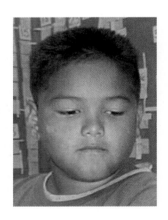

Faces are rarely exactly symmetrical. Get a full-face photo of yourself, family members, and friends. And find full-face photos of famous people in magazines. Place a mirror right between the eyes on the photos to see what the people would look like if their faces were exactly symmetrical. How do the right and left sides compare?

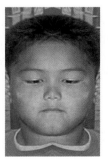
Left side

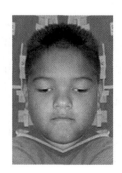
Right side

Make a Periscope

A periscope is a tube with a mirror at each end. It works because light travels in a straight line. But you can use mirrors to change the direction of the light. In a periscope, the far mirror points at an object. Light from the object reflects off the far mirror. The light bounces onto the closer mirror and then into the eyes of the observer. Make a periscope and use it to see over walls and around corners.

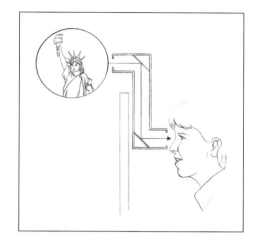

Determine Volume of Solid Objects

Solid objects like apples have volumes. But their volumes can't be measured directly with 50-mL syringes and graduated cylinders. One way to measure the volume of a solid object is to use water displacement. You can measure the volume of water an object displaces (pushes out) from a full container.

a. Use scissors to cut the top off a 2-liter soda bottle 16 cm up from its base.

b. Make a spillway in the displacement vessel. Do this by making two 5-cm cuts that angle toward each other. The cuts should start 6 cm apart and end up 2 cm apart. This forms a flap.

c. Bend the flap down. That's it.

To use the displacement vessel, set it in a basin or sink. Place a 1/2-liter container under the flap. Fill the vessel with water until it overflows. The flap will direct the overflow into the 1/2-liter container. When the water stops overflowing, carefully remove the 1/2-liter container. Empty the container and return it to its catch position.

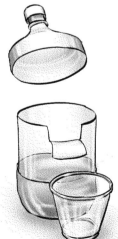

Now place an object in the vessel. The object will displace water equal to its own volume. (If an object floats, push it under water with your finger.) Measure the water that was displaced to determine the volume of the solid object.

Conservation of Matter

The baking soda-and-vinegar reaction produces a gas. The gas escapes into the air. This results in a net loss of mass in the reaction cup. Use a closed system to see if the mass is the same before and after the reaction. You will need a medium-size balloon and an empty plastic drinking-water bottle.

a. Place 5 milliliters of baking soda in the balloon and 50 milliliters of vinegar in the bottle.

b. Pull the balloon over the bottle. Make sure no baking soda spills into the vinegar yet.

c. Place the system on one side of a balance. Place mass pieces on the other side to balance the scale.

d. With the balloon system still in the balance, pull the balloon straight up. This will spill the baking soda into the bottle. Make sure the balloon stays on the bottle.

e. Observe the balloon inflate.

f. Weigh the system and compare the final mass to the starting mass.

Baking soda

Vinegar

FOSSweb

Go to www.FOSSweb.com to find activities for each FOSS module. You will also find interesting books to read, vocabulary lists, and links to related websites. This site was designed for you to use with friends and family at home. For your parents, there is information about each FOSS module and copies of the Home/School Connections.

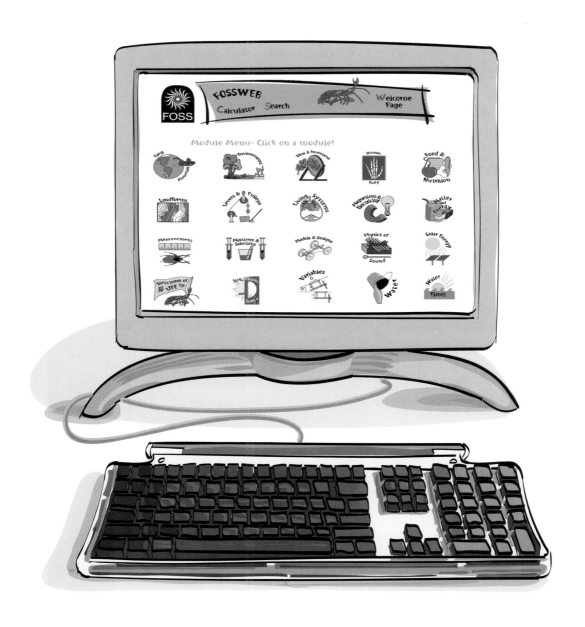

Science Safety Rules

1. Listen carefully to your teacher's instructions. Follow all directions. Ask questions if you don't know what to do.

2. Tell your teacher if you have any allergies.

3. Never put any materials in your mouth. Do not taste anything unless your teacher tells you to do so.

4. Never smell any unknown material. If your teacher tells you to smell something, wave your hand over the material to bring the smell toward your nose.

5. Do not touch your face, mouth, ears, eyes, or nose while working with chemicals, plants, or animals.

6. Always protect your eyes. Wear safety goggles when necessary. Tell your teacher if you wear contact lenses.

7. Always wash your hands with soap and warm water after handling chemicals, plants, or animals.

8. Never mix any chemicals unless your teacher tells you to do so.

9. Report all spills, accidents, and injuries to your teacher.

10. Treat animals with respect, caution, and consideration.

11. Clean up your work space after each investigation.

12. Act responsibly during all science activities.

Glossary

Absorb To take in or soak up.

Accurate Very close to the correct answer.

Battery A source of stored chemical energy.

Chemical energy Energy stored in a substance.

Convert To change.

Electric current A flow of electricity through a wire.

Electricity A form of energy that can be converted to other forms of energy, such as heat, light, and sound.

Energy The ability to make things happen. Energy can take a number of forms and can be converted from one form to another.

Energy source A place where energy comes from, such as batteries, food, fuels, and the Sun.

Evaporate To change from liquid to gas.

Evidence Data used to support claims. Evidence is based on observation and scientific data.

Food The energy source that keeps things alive.

Fossil The preserved remains of plants and animals that lived long ago.

Fossil fuel The preserved remains of plants that lived long ago and changed into oil, coal, and natural gas.

Fuel A material that contains energy.

Gas   Matter that is shapeless and expands to fill a closed container.

Generator   A device that converts motion into electric energy.

Gram (g)   The basic unit of mass in the metric system.

Heat   A form of energy.

Light   A form of energy.

Light source   Anything that makes light, such as the Sun, a lightbulb, or a flame.

Liquid   Matter that flows and takes the shape of the container it is in.

Liter (L)   The basic unit of liquid volume in the metric system.

Mass   A quantity of matter.

Matter   Anything that has mass and takes up space.

Melt   To change from solid to liquid. Heat causes solids to melt.

Meter (m)   The basic unit of distance or length in the metric system.

Metric system   A measuring system based on multiples of ten.

Mirror   A shiny surface that reflects an image.

Motion   A form of energy.

Motor   A device that converts electric energy into motion energy.

Moving object   An object that is changing position.

Opinion A claim based on belief, not on scientific data or observations.

Particle The smallest building blocks of matter.

Periscope A device with two mirrors used to change the path taken by light.

Property A characteristic of an object, such as size, shape, and texture.

Ray A line of light that travels straight out from a light source.

Reaction An interaction between substances that produces one or more new substances that have different properties than the starting substances.

Reflect To bounce off an object or surface.

Shaft The part of a motor that spins.

Solid Matter that has a definite shape.

Sound A form of energy carried by sound waves.

Sound wave A wave produced by the energy of a vibrating object.

State A form of matter. The three common states of matter are solid, liquid, and gas.

Stored energy Energy available for use.

Substance Matter that can be defined by the particles from which it is made.

Sun The star around which Earth orbits. The Sun provides energy to Earth.

Synthetic Something that is made by humans.

Temperature   A measure of how hot a sample of matter is.

Vibrate   To move back-and-forth quickly.

Vibration   A quick back-and-forth movement.

Volume   Three-dimensional space.

Water vapor   Water in its gas state.

Water wave   A wave carrying the energy of moving water.

Wave   A regular, repeating pattern, such as an ocean wave or a sound wave.

White light   Light that is all colors mixed together.

Wind   Air in motion.

Wire   A strand of metal through which electric energy can move.

Index

Photo Credits